The Edge of Africa's Eden

by
Harmon Schmelzenbach

Nazarene Publishing House
Kansas City, Missouri

Copyright 1991
by Nazarene Publishing House

ISBN: 083-411-3899

Printed in the
United States of America

Cover Design: Royce Ratcliff

Permission to quote from *The Holy Bible, New International Version* (NIV), copyright
© 1973, 1978, 1984 by the International Bible Society, is acknowledged with
appreciation.

10   9   8   7   6   5   4   3   2   1

Dedicated to the three people
who gave me their best.

Mary Schmelzenbach,
for all her love as a mother.

Wade and Helen Gustin, who gave
me the girl that I took with me to

AFRICA

Contents

Will the Moon Be OK?	7
1 / Across the Serengeti	9
Plains of East Africa • Tribal Settlement • Geology of Rift Valley • Volcanoes • Nairobi	
2 / Lateen Sails and Arab Dwohs	16
People of the Coast • The Slave Trade • The Coming of Missionaries • Disease and Death • In the Steps of Livingstone • Change	
3 / On the Damascus Road	23
Kenya Assignment • Survey • Registration • God's Promise • Funds • Bethany First Church • Leaving Namibia • Innovative Planning	
4 / Bushfire and High Wind on the Equator	28
Market Services • Teaching Conferences • No Subsidy	
5 / Blowing Sand and Camels	39
Compassionate Ministries • Ethiopia • Kenya Office and Scope	
6 / Did Not Our Hearts Burn Within Us?	48
The Planning of the Seminary • Training of the Preachers • Gastineau, Anderson—Team Concept	
7 / The Tools of Leadership	59
Esselstyn • Land • General Board • Zanner • Roles, Swaziland College • Calling Moore • Hayse, Work and Witness • Johnson, Marangu	
8 / The Men with the Spears	72
Growth Rate • Central Church • Scott, Tanzania, Mission Director, New District, University • Future	

Will the Moon Be OK?

The tropical moon was full and bright. The typical night sounds of Africa were all around. In the big baobab tree a hundred yards away, I heard the cry of a bushbaby. It sounded for all the world like a baby lost in the night. Close by, a nightjar called repeatedly his three-note call. In the distance a turtledove started to coo and then stopped suddenly.

My son, Harmon, and his wife, Cindy, stood in the bright moonlight with me. Beside us was the dark form of a tall Maasai holding a spear. The beach lay before us, and the silver of the still ocean sparkled in the moonlight. As we watched, a shadow slowly started to form along one side of the full moon. It moved across the edge of brightness, covering the light. The Maasai watched in stunned silence. The shadow of the earth moved slowly over the surface of the moon, and it became very dark.

"Will the moon be OK, Bwana?"

I waited a moment, and a sliver of light started to appear along the edge of the dark moon. I replied softly, "Yes, my friend, it will all be OK."

This century has shaken the foundations of ancient Africa. God is still on His throne, and He does not change. All will be OK if placed in His eternal hand!

1

Across the Serengeti

From the crest of the low, rocky hills, I gazed out over an incredible sight. As far as I could see, the earth rippled with the movement of a million animals. They poured from the south to the north, and the stream never seemed to end. The white stripes of the zebra stood out in contrast to the dark coats of the gnu. A hundred thousand wildebeests, ebbing and flowing like the tide, blended into the sea of life.

It was like a stage so big that it ran from heaven to the ends of the earth; green backdrop; darker, flat-topped thorn trees with yellow trunks. The folds and ridges of earth were all covered with life on the move. I watched with the fascination that Adam and a million of his children must have had. Their spears, bows and arrows in their hands, children of Africa, all.

This was the Serengeti as I first saw it. Nature, with a sweep as great as creation, spilling out the final performance of a play that dated back to the beginning of time.

The lioness broke from cover at a dead run. Every time she touched ground her speed increased. She ran smoothly as she closed in on the two giraffes. They were moving down the slope straight toward me at full gallop—a tall, full-grown female giraffe and a small, furry calf. She rose and dipped as if in slow motion, but I knew that every time her hooves touched ground she had moved 25 feet. Behind her, head held high, the young one ran for its life. Spindly legs flying, tail twisted up on its back, and every young muscle straining, it fled across the green grass down the slope.

They were a hundred feet away from me now. The lioness reached forward, touched the small giraffe on the flank, and it fell. With the agility of a bounding impala, the mother changed her direction in full stride. A ton and a half of towering giraffe swung completely around, and her baby slid under her. The lion was sliding on its side scrambling to regain its feet. The giraffe's 12-inch giant hooves rose together 10 feet above the lioness and came down. In a second the roles were reversed. The angry mother lunged forward and the lioness ran for her life across the open grass, barely making it to the thick bushes ahead of the giraffe.

Close by the baby unfolded himself and rose on his wobbly legs. He swung his furry little head and watched the drama with large, dark eyes. In a few seconds the mother was back, and the little one fell in behind her at a full gallop. Together they swayed down the slope toward the trees along the river.

The members of the Work and Witness team I was guiding broke into wild cheers. I laughed. For them it was so new, for me it was a drama played over with a hundred variations during my 55 years in Africa.

My mind flashed back to that early morning two days before my 12th birthday when I met my first lion. The dusty smell of dry grass filled my memory. My whole world had shaken with the terrifying roar of that huge, angry lion coming for me.

I could recall every detail in slow motion. The small bird gun that I carried for guinea fowl was as cold and light as a pencil in my hand. I was swinging it and pointing. There was a moving blur beyond the site on the front of my gun. Then the sounds, like no thunder I had ever heard. Roar upon roar . . . terror! Yellow eyes blazed before me, and I heard the small sound of my gun. The lion,

10 feet away, was sinking and then rolling. He was down! Down flat! Move, move, move!

A hand was on my shoulder, "You OK?" asked the broad accent.

"Yes, yes," I replied. "Just caught up with that young giraffe. Guess we all face it sometime."

"Yeah, guess so." Still talking, we climbed into the minibus. The sharp taste of adrenalin still in my mouth, we bounced down the trail to our tents.

Sometime later I approached a village at dusk. The day had been long and hard, and the drifting, blue smoke from the low shelter of the stockade was welcome. It was a large settlement and contained all of the old man's extended family. In this remote area I was sure that he had faced the same problems of cattle raids and attacks that his ancestors had faced. Otherwise, the family would have broken up, and many of them would have gone to the great city of Nairobi.

The men were outside the brush stockade in several groups helping bring in the cattle for the night. Dust hung thickly over the scene, and the heat of the day was just beginning to lift. The shouts of the men and boys were muted by the lowing of cows seeking their calves and the bleating of goats who stood aside as if shy, watching the larger animals barge toward the openings in the poles and brush.

A long line of women and girls wound their way up the slope from the river carrying bright yellow and white plastic containers filled with water. Their shrill voices drifted up to me through the surrounding din. I walked up to the old flat-topped tree that formed the official outer meeting area of the village. I waited there for someone to greet me and invite me closer. There were many large rocks, and I sat down on one to wait.

Soon several of the older men worked their way over, and one by one, they greeted me. One of them seated himself close to me and started the long greeting. What news did I bear?

"All good!" was the standard response. I studied the thin, slender face with high cheekbones and larger earlobes that had been cut to hang in great open circles against his neck. He nodded and smiled and waited for me to put the same question to him. Slowly, one question and answer at a time, we worked our way through the formalities.

How was his wife and family? His cattle? The rains? and a dozen other topics. I spoke of my travels and the land I had passed through. It took a full hour. The tropical light was fading before I spoke of the truck that was stuck in the dry sand of the riverbed and the help I would need tomorrow to get free. This was the speed of urgency in an African village, even in the 20th century.

The Maasai were latecomers in this new world of mine. They had poured down out of the north sometime in the past. They had followed the Nile into the heart of the continent, driving their herds of cattle and sweeping the weaker tribes before them. They were one of the few pastoral people on the earth. They lived with and on their stock. Much of their diet was warm milk mixed with blood, drawn each day from the necks of the cattle. Traditionally, they did not plow or eat grain. "God had given the cattle of the earth to them and them only." In their minds that is what made it all right to raid and recover cattle wherever they found them. If one brought home a few of the women too, so be it. When the grazing was poor, they simply moved on and followed the rain.

Fear was a word they never knew. Death was honorable if it came in battle, but few tribes wished to prove the point. Not even the Arab slavers took them on, in spite of the modern weapons they carried across Africa as they collected their human cargo.

A friend of mine watched a dozen young warriors hunting a lion one day. They didn't see him in the truck as he bounced down the track along the river. The lion was a large male with a thick yellow mane and a swollen belly full of meat. He came bounding across the track before my friend saw the warriors. The lion never saw him but kept running into the long grass. Wild with frenzy, and glistening silver with sweat, the group of young Maasai swept over the track 50 feet behind the lion. They were screaming, and they saw nothing.

The first young man bounded into the tall grass right behind the lion. His face was set, and his sharp features looked like black marble. Long hair, red with ocher, swung over his shoulders. His light red cloak trailed behind his naked body across the muscles of his back. His trailing arm swept forward driven by all his weight, and he drove his four-foot spear into the lion just in front of the flank. He thrust it in until the turning animal caught him with open claws, spinning the young warrior head over heels into the dust. He didn't move. A second warrior drove his spear into the ground, leapt forward, and grabbed the lion's tail. The lion was thrown off balance, and in that instant, the rest of the warriors were on him. Boldly they drove their spears through and through the lion, pinning him to the ground, snarling and coughing.

In less than a minute it was over, and the legs of the lion stretched and shook and then fell soft. But the men didn't stop. Their eyes wild, and the froth flicking from the corners of their mouths, they struck the lion repeatedly until still shouting they dropped to the ground exhausted. Those who were hurt felt nothing, and the first young man with the gaping wounds was sitting and shouting like the rest, covered in blood. He beckoned, and another warrior severed the tail and threw it to him. The prize was his! Hopefully, he would live long enough to show it to the girl he was courting. My friend let out the clutch and bounced on. He had glimpsed the wild Africa of the past.

The great Rift Valley lay before me. The grazing land of the Maasai was ahead and far below. Two thousand feet below, villages dotted the floor of the plain. Fifty miles away the land rose again as ridges and valleys lay in endless parallel folds. A thousand miles to the west, the far side of the earth plate pushed up the mountains, and the fractures opened for volcanoes that threw fire and smoke skyward, from deep under Africa.

We looked down on a vast green blanket with tiny villages and men far below. Once, this had been fire too. Thirty miles away rose an ancient volcano with its gaping crater and deep ridges cut by falling mud and water. To the south was the peak of Kilimanjaro, nearly four miles high. Further south were other great mountains, their day of fear and thunder past.

The Nile rose in Lake Victoria, 300 miles west of here. With water came life, and early traces of it were found in stone arrowheads and axes along the shores of these lakes. A little to the south was a great flat rock, baked by volcanic heat from ash and mud. Across the rock, among the thousands of animal and bird tracks, there were three sets of bare human footprints. They are small and about the size of a present-day Bushman's. One is the footprint of a man, the others are those of a woman and child. They walked out across that ancient mud flat and at one point stood and turned to look back. Their footprints are engraved in rock today. They date back to when? Was it soon after God walked with Adam?

A black eagle swept past and below me and several hundred feet out from the crest of the escarpment of the Great Rift

Valley. He was balanced on the wind, and only the slight movement of a wingtip feather showed that he was master of his movements. On a rock ledge a thousand feet below, a rock rabbit dozed in the warm sunlight.

The eagle turned up on edge and folded his wings. He swept downward like a shaft of shadow. It took only seconds, and before the coney could open his eyes, the wingtips of the eagle flared and the talons dropped a little. The trailing claw entered the rabbit on the back and split him open to the head. He died without knowing the danger or fear. The fall broken, the eagle looped upward and back down onto the rock beside the prey it had caught. He cocked his head and then reached down and started to feed.

Within an hour I was parking in downtown Nairobi. No easy task, it usually involves several people, all volunteers. A young man dressed in checkered pants and a blue T-shirt with the logo "DOWN WITH THE WALL" across his chest, stepped out in front of my slow-moving car. He glanced at me through his large and very dark "shades" and raised his hand for me to stop. Turning he started beckoning to the car parked behind him. Red brake lights came on and then a white backup light, and very hesitantly the car squeezed out. The wheels locked in a tight right turn, he pulled into the lane. I had won my share for the day. A parking place in Nairobi, and it cost me five shillings to have the young city warrior guard my car from a parking ticket until I came back.

This was East Africa and some of my impressions and feelings of it. The Church of the Nazarene had chosen to enter this part of the world a month before Christmas at the end of 1984. I would learn it and its people well in the years that God would give.

2

Lateen Sails and Arab Dwohs

Once or twice a year I try to get away and spend a week or so at the Mombasa Coast. I am usually awake to welcome dawn when I am there. Far out to sea there is always a low cloud bank, so the sun is seldom seen until a few seconds after dawn breaks. First there is a golden shaft of light cutting through the mauve banks of low cloud. Almost immediately, the edge of an orange sun appears and then disappears through the banks of cloud. At last it rises above them swiftly, and the top turns bright gold. A few seconds later it becomes too bright to watch. It is witnessing the birth of a fresh new day that is best of all.

Thirty yards out, a log canoe glides past. Two men, black silhouettes against the bright gold, lean in unison on their poles—bend and push, bend and push. There is no sound of their passing. Only a shimmering gold line spreading out behind them in small waves.

The tide is at ebb, and there are no breaking waves on the inside of the reef. Only a small sloshing moves the foam a foot or so on the sand.

At my feet, in yesterday's footprints and tumbled down sand castles, pale ghost crabs edge sideways hesitantly. With a heavy claw, they reach out and pick at the thin lines of sea grass left behind by the tide. Suddenly, at some imagined danger, they scatter sideways, scurrying out of sight into holes in the fine white sand, only to emerge again and sit on the edge of the hole, lifting first one eye stalk and then another to check and see where the fear came from and where the neighbor is.

Closer to the water's edge, a crab is slowly moving a wedge of washed-up orange peel, turning it over and reaching out with a large claw to sample it. The chill of the night disappears within a minute as the warm sun rises, shaking itself loose from the highest of the cloud banks. The sea starts to respond and awaken with a faraway sound of wave breaking on reef. Day has come again, the time for the men to head out to sea.

By afternoon the sail was just a small patched ivory triangle that jerked and swung from side to side. Every point strained in the wind. The deep log canoe hid the three Swahili men in it up to their waists. As each wave caught them from behind, the back of the canoe rose and raced forward.

Perched on the support poles of the outrigger, a foot above the racing green water and foam, sat the boy. In his hand was the thin line streaming out behind him with the small hook and bright feather. He was almost a man now and could swing the sail and lift it and the long log to which it was tied. He was as good as they at flipping a loose loop of rope out to the end of the outrigger to pull the sail tight.

With one leg out sideways, he squatted on the outrigger pole and leaned against the sail rope. He swept his hand back and forth to move the feather. In the wet wicker basket down in the bottom of the boat, a dozen pewter-gray ocean bonito and a small yellow-fin tuna shared space. It had been a good day, and home was only an hour downwind.

As dusk swiftly descended on the men and the boy, they pulled the deep canoe across the sand and onto the grass under the coconut trees. The sail was wrapped around the pole with the rope twisted around it. Two of them lifted it and started toward the huts a hundred yards away. The small children shouted around them.

At the huts they pushed the sail up onto an old coral stone wall among the overgrown vines. A bright fire crackled in the yard, and a tall woman with an orange and brown cloth around her waist busied herself around the fire. The men were home again. The day was done.

In the darkness below the sail and pole, the coral wall dropped away onto a pit a dozen feet down. Thousands of clam shells lay in piles in the dark recesses along the wall, a testament to many feasts under full moons.

Against the dull white of the coral wall hung more than 50 rusted iron rings. This ancient wall, where the children climbed and jumped each day, had once been owned by slave traders. A hundred thousand men, women, and children had died here in misery.

The slave traffic nearly depopulated the entire interior of central Africa. Chiefs were constantly selling the captives of tribal wars. This traffic was supplemented by the well-armed caravans of Arab slave catchers and traders. The flow of humanity numbered millions, but the flow went one way only.

Great fortunes were made by the Sultan of Zanzibar until the warships of the British empire appeared and the trade ended. It was along those bone-lined trails into the interior of Africa that the feet of Livingstone and a hundred others like him had trod. The sound of British cannons over the water was the direct result of the courage of these men to return to England and be heard on the issue of the day. Gaunt, fever-yellowed men whose eyes shone with the holy light of a mission to "heal the open sore of the world."

Many of the missionaries of Freetown had died at the hands of the slavers. The great bell that rang every time the sails of the slavers' ships were seen, now hung silent on a monument in Mombasa. The open slave market on Zanzibar closed forever on the 5th of June 1873.

With the passing of the slave trade came the colonizing of Africa. Before the turn of the century, iron rails had started out across wild bush country. By 1901 Lake Victoria was joined to Mombasa. A small rail stop along the way was named Nairobi.

The first automobile came to this part of Africa in 1907. It was a little 35-horse, four cylinder belonging to Paul Graetz. He had driven it straight west across Africa to Ujiji, then to the town of Livingstone and on to Bulawayo and Johannesburg. As there were no roads, he followed the elephant trails most of the way. From there he crossed the Kalahari westward to Windhoek and reached the Atlantic on May 1, 1909, at Swakopmund. It took 2 years for the car to cover almost all the terrain that Livingstone had walked across for 35 years.

In the year 1928 when my grandfather left Africa to speak at the General Assembly, the first regular air service started between East Africa and London.

Today the caravan routes past Kilimanjaro to the interior are paved, and they thunder with 18-wheel trucks. The lonely mission stations are now absorbed into sprawling markets and small, untidy towns. These towns were built around clinics and hospitals and schools that were the stepping-stones of history as Africa awoke into the 20th century. The missionary of today, in his Bronco or Blazer or his Cessna 206, working on some unwritten language with his Apple or IBM, is also changing fast. Today he is often a son of Africa with a degree from "Fuller" or "Moody" or "Olivet." His face shows tribal scars be-neath his glasses. Often he is black instead of white, and he has a deep interest in the salvation of his continent.

In Kenya, it has been within the last century and a half all that we call "MISSIONS" has occurred. The first missionaries to East Africa were incredibly brave men and women. God had called them to an unknown place.

After arriving, there was a good chance they would be eaten. Lions and tribesmen did it equally well! And they had a day-by-day battle with malaria, cholera, yellow fever, leprosy, yaws, bilharziasis, elephantiasis, gas gangrene, and a hundred other maladies. In Kenya, cannibals had never been a problem. There had been some, but they came up out of the south along the coast and soon ate themselves out of house and home and had to return. Deeper into the continent, however, there were areas where cannibalism was practiced.

Disease is still a major factor. The five types of malaria still head the list. Only recently have we learned that there are several types of mosquitoes that carry malaria. We also know that DDT cannot be used to save the situation. Millions die in Africa each year. Missionary Dan Anderson suffered from malaria twice in one year, and his little preschool son had it once. Only prayer and the help of a menu of new drugs has kept them alive.

Those missionaries that came early did not fare so well. One of the first who landed at Mombasa Island buried his wife and three children within three months. Their moss-covered graves lie on a bluff on the mainland north of the island. The father alone survived and spent the rest of his life working in East Africa. He and a fellow missionary were the first Europeans to see the snows of the great Kilimanjaro. He translated the Bible into the vernacular and, in order to do so, put the local language into writing. He reached many tribes inland and left mission stations that stand today as lighthouses.

It was missionaries in most cases who drew the map of the interior of Africa. On some lonely rock-covered hill, under the flat thorn trees, I have from time to time found their graves. Sometimes they are unmarked except for a pile of stones. Sometimes there is a small cracked and broken piece of cement with a cross and name followed by a date.

It was Rev. Rebmann of the Church Mission Society who, on May 11, 1848, became the first to record that there was a mountain nearly 20,000 feet high with eternal ice and snow on it not far off the equator of Africa. Rev. Charles New, another missionary, was the first to climb to the summit through the snow.

A fellow missionary called Livingstone recorded a great river plunging over a thundering falls more than a mile wide. The Africans called it "the smoke that thunders." He named it Victoria Falls in honor of his queen.

The missionaries were not in these distant and remote places to record and explore. They were there to tell men living there that Christ died on a cross for them. Nothing turned those with a call of God aside from that purpose. I stood beside one of the great evangelists of our denomination some time back. We were in Africa at a Nazarene mission station standing under the trees. The grave of a missionary and three of his children lay in the dappled sunlight at our feet. "I've preached all over the world," he said, "and I've been hosted in every great city of America. I've spoken at the General Assemblies of our church and heard all the nice things people say about me. But if you ever need to be brought down to size, come and stand right here where I now stand, where this man built his altar and made his sacrifice for the King."

In my office I have a prized inheritance. It is a simple upright bookcase. It consists of five straight shelves and two single plank upright ends. The shelves have ears that come through the ends, and then in each ear is a peg driven down to hold it there. In an age of materialism and fancy gadgets, it is nothing really. Except that it is all hand-carved with a pocket knife and was all that my grandfather could give to my grandmother for Christmas in Swaziland the year that they lost their first child. When my fax or IBM or air-conditioned 4 x 4 station wagon gives me a problem, that bookcase reminds me that I am not bound by the limits of modern technology in carrying out my calling. In modern times, missionary work has adopted modern methods. We are careful, however, not to "remove the ancient landmarks" erected by the great men and women that went before us.

Up the street from where I live in Nairobi is an apartment block. It houses half a dozen volunteer families of highly qualified Nazarene professors and other professional people. They pay their own way and give their own time and money to help carry the gospel to Kenya. Yes, today it is different from the day of the pioneers of the last century. Yet I see the same spirit of sacrifice and love that has always distinguished the true disciple. May God help us to always keep it so!

3

On the Damascus Road

The phone rang in the office of the district superintendent in Houston. It was late January 1984. I was on a special tour of selected U.S. districts at the request of Dr. L. Guy Nees. My wife, Beverly, had remained in Namibia, and I had flown to the States for seven weeks. No deputation was involved. Dr. D. Thaxton handed the phone to me. "It's for you," he said. On the other end of the line was Dr. Richard Zanner. He had been appointed the regional director for the African continent two years before. At his urging, I had decided to undertake this special tour for the Department of World Mission.

"Harmon, I'm at the General Board in Kansas City, and there are two things that I want to share with you. The first is that the board has just approved our going into five new world areas. I've secured two of those for Africa. They have approved our entering Botswana." He chuckled. He already knew that in 1970 I had registered the Church of the Nazarene in Botswana. I had paid the registration fee personally and with great joy. No one knew how many trips I had made across that beautiful land and the Kalahari. Both he and many other missionaries had gone with me and sat around the campfires with the little Bushmen there. Now what he was saying was that we could get the funds to follow through and open it up.

Dr. Zanner paused and said, "The other area is East Africa. This is not a country. The work there is to be started in Kenya and springboarded from that country into Uganda, Tanzania, and the other countries. I have called to ask you if you would go begin the work."

My mind raced. Beverly was 10,000 miles away. Our home in Namibia had a complete house full of furniture from the States. The house had been renovated with many hours of night work by the two of us. For the first time, we had full carpeting that we had bought and laid ourselves. I had built a kitchen breakfast bar out of red brick and set a glass-top stove in it. A wall oven and overhead cabinets had been my last project.

The last of our three children had come to the States for college. The work on the house was partly my way of trying to fill the gap in our lives and hearts. Our house was now a home. People came in often for Bible study and coffee. The church was growing. I knew, of course, what Beverly would say. Her choice had been made many years ago. I had never seen the slightest hesitancy in the 25 years that we had served on the field.

As soon as I landed back in Africa, I flew to see Dr. Zanner. Plans were made without making my assignment public. I asked him to request two of the missionaries that would travel that way soon, to stop over in Kenya and do some survey work in different aspects of missionary work. Based on the information they gave, I decided to go to work on the registration. I also decided to visit most of the country and survey it for myself.

What a visit it was. In four weeks I traveled several thousand miles in small public vehicles called "Matatu's." For the most part they were small half-ton pickups with a metal roof over the bed. They were licensed to carry 22 people and seldom carried less. Time was money, and they waited for no one.

We moved with unbroken speed. On the narrow highway, we formed a third fast lane over the white line between the oncoming fuel tanker and trailer and next to the 18 wheeler. Lights flashed and the screams of passengers were lost in the blast of air horns and the thunder of great tires on both sides.

In market after market I spoke to thousands of people about their souls. To my surprise, a missionary in Nairobi had assured me that most Kenyans already "knew the Lord" and we really were not needed here but should find somewhere where no work had been done. My questions to the people gave a very different picture. Yes, the people knew of Christ, but few knew Him as Savior in their lives.

They suffered from the many ills of sin. Theft, graft, immorality, and crime were all part of the big city scene. From surveying the people, I soon learned that many areas of the country needed us if we could gain the registration we sought.

Back in Nairobi a month later, I spoke to a law firm and applied for registration as an international denomination. This would allow the international church to hold all the property without fear of losing it to some individual. However, it would not be easy to gain registration without some existing denomination sponsoring or giving us their registration as an umbrella for several years. In fact, one church leader wrote me that it would be impossible.

We filed for registration and then returned home to wait. Several months passed and letters came and went between the lawyers and myself. The Kenya government was aware of what Nazarenes had done on the African continent in other countries, and I updated them. Then one day the impossible occurred. I opened a letter, and there was the registration for the Church of the Nazarene to operate in Kenya.

We left for Kenya within days. A container was packed

and shipped the same week. In it went a welder, building tools, overhead saw, complete overhaul tools for my car and trucks. There was our old bed that had come to Africa with us years ago, and the matching dresser. All the new furniture stayed behind.

I have often said that the Lord promised us a "legion of angels" to help us in the opening of the new work. In retrospect, it had to be so. There was no other way to explain the growth.

At dusk we looked out of the plane window from 35,000 feet at the setting sun on the snows of Kilimanjaro. Soon we landed, and the tires squawked on the runway in the tropical night. In the backseat of an old cab, we bowed our heads and the Master spoke of promise and courage. There was no one to welcome us, of course, and we asked the driver to take us to an inexpensive hotel. We made it our home for several weeks until we could rent something. We were not far from downtown and could walk back and forth every day.

During these first days, we started the intensives for the training of pastors. We wanted full participation and as much exposure and training as possible, so we offered to pay the travel expenses of the men to and from the conferences. In the four years of the program, we had a high percentage of preachers attend all of the conferences.

In the second and third year, we started a parallel home training program. Rev. Dan Anderson did the bulk of this training and found it to be a very good method. However, the lack of missionaries with free time made it impossible to continue during the past two years. Dr. Al Jones has recently been assigned to implement home training into the current educational program. The financing of all of these new programs and training areas was met entirely by gifts from involved Nazarene laymen. Steve and Myla, friends of ours that own a ranch, provided much of this. Funds given by Bethany First Church in Oklahoma City started it. Later, much of it came from the deputation offerings that were raised on the short furloughs that we took. It was a great miracle!

In trying to find ways to make the work grow at the fastest possible pace, we did everything to use all our resources. For instance, when building started on outstation churches, we needed a truck for hauling. We had no funds to purchase one. So, by using some deputation funds, Roger and I got hold of an old truck chassis. Then we found a drive train that looked good. One of the truck dealers in town put it all together and mounted the cab. We hired a firm to make a truck bed. In no time we had a truck that has served until the present. It is a four-cylinder diesel and woefully underpowered, but it has struggled along and now there are churches and four college buildings because of a minimal investment in a truck.

4

Bushfire and High Wind on the Equator

The very first services were held almost immediately. We had many persons calling at the door seeking work, and in no time, word spread that there were new people in the house that we had rented. We had inherited a man who worked in the yard, and we asked him to invite those he knew to come in for a service in the evening. Beverly made coffee and cake.

The room was full in a week, and these people all knew of some place where they wanted us to go and preach. Among the first people to start coming was a young man by the name of Alfred. He became my interpreter. Alfred knew the entire city well and soon led me into the suburbs of Kibera. There we preached in the open market for a long while until the rains forced us to rent a room and start a congregation. Two years later, Alfred became the pastor of that church.

We went from one place to the next in similar fashion. Everyone knew some other place where they had friends, and they wanted us to preach there. In short order there were six regular congregations in the Nairobi area and a growing group of young men who followed us from meeting to meeting, helping with the services. I spent hours talking with them and teaching them.

Beverly had been given some puppets and used them in

the open-air services. They were a great help in winning friends. Both kids and adults came from all around and sat spellbound while she told stories from the Bible using the puppets. Each puppet had a name, and soon the kids knew all of them. They would call for the one they wanted by name to tell its story. There was laughter and fun, and the move into preaching was easy and friendly.

It was not long until April rains arrived with a vengeance! The rivers were flooded, and the trails into the areas where we were holding services became a bottomless swamp. Seventy-eight people drowned within the Nairobi city limits that year.

When we arrived in Kenya, we bought a four-wheel-drive station wagon called a Trooper, which we quickly put to the test. I spent much of the time in four-wheel drive inside the city limits! In typical African fashion, we never left home without a full load of people. Everyone was interested and wanted to go along ... and I needed the push power! So it was crowded but effective. There is nothing like bare human feet when it comes to pushing in slick clay mud. The problem here was that across this part of the world the soil was largely volcanic ash. It is fine and slick, and when it is wet, one has to hold onto the car just to remain upright. Somehow we made it through, and in the process, we got to know each other very well indeed.

In Kibera, we rented a small room and crammed in more than a hundred men, women, and children. In other places it was not that easy. The fact that no budget had yet been assigned to Kenya, and funds were not plentiful, did not add to the solutions. We could not afford to rent schools or social halls if they were available, and they seldom were. In one instance, we tried a social hall and found that there were six other services going on at the same time, and no soundproofing. The problem with home services was that in no time at all we had outgrown the home. So, if possible, we met outside in the sunshine and only moved inside when all else failed.

It was not the easiest thing to get urban people to settle down and become faithful to the church. We won them to Christ, but there were hundreds of other groups meeting everywhere. The Church of the Nazarene had no permanent buildings or even loyal pastors, so the turnover was great, and real growth in the city was slow. In fact, only two of the six churches grew into strong congregations that retained over a hundred regular adherents. In time, this problem will be solved by the adequate training of good ministers with pastoral skills and permanent buildings.

Many good men came into the ministry as a result of the services across western Kenya, but something had to be done to pull the men together and start training them in a more formal way. I had been visiting them and talking with them in their homes. I sought a meeting place and finally decided on the YMCA. Several dozen men took time from home and work and came in for three weeks. Dr. Ted Esselstyn came and taught them, and it was a great time of unity and spiritual fellowship.

The beginning of an organization took place with lessons on the *Manual,* doctrine, and how to keep books and reports, and many other things that make up a denomination. As we prayed together, the men started searching for a deeper walk with Christ. Some took a step of faith that led to their sanctification. The total cost of the conference, which incidentally earned each person five educational credits, was around $5,000. This included flying Dr. Esselstyn in and paying all the costs of the men who came and stayed the entire time. We continued doing this training program for four years—up until the seminary was able to take in the first students. At that time, the responsibility for the training of preachers fell on the institution.

By this time, there was a great deal of speculation and curiosity among Nazarene missionaries in other areas about what was happening in Kenya. Following the intensives, Dr. Esselstyn returned to the regional office. He was bombarded with questions. His response was simply, "I have run out of superlatives." As he was not known for his orations, this did much to gather support for the new work developing in East Africa.

In the years to follow, the response of the preachers never failed to stagger the key teachers that were invited to teach at the pastors' intensives. When they walked into the hall where a hundred new Nazarene preachers stood to greet them, they were impressed. God was doing some good thing here.

Among those who shared in this vital teaching ministry were Dr. Ken Walker and Dr. Hal Cauthron from Swaziland Bible College, Dr. Bill Prince from Mount Vernon, Dr. Glen Kell from Zambia, and many others. Our local missionaries took up the slack, and some taught in almost all the conferences. Leo Mpoke taught in all of them, and near the end, we flew in a final-year Kenya student, Wellington Obotte, to give classes. It was a morale booster for the men to see one of their own come back well trained.

By the end of the second conference, I was convinced that we would need to separate and train the men in several different ways to enable them to prepare as quickly as possible. Consequently, two groups were sent by air to the Bible college in Swaziland, about six months apart. Several followed at other times.

I wanted them to absorb the heritage by seeing the Church in Swaziland where it all started on the African continent, so long ago. Particularly, I wanted them to see the self-supporting national church, running its own work without a great missionary infusion. I wanted them to see our strong, well-established denomination and the African laymen who were members of parliament and ministers in government. This would provide a needed role model.

The plan to send Kenyans to Swaziland was successful, but it was not without pain. There was a large cultural gap between the multi-tribal Kenya students and the local tribal community. By tradition, the local people were extremely courteous. The Kenya students came from a society that was highly competitive. If one was not aggressive, one stood no chance of making it in Kenya. So at the close of a lecture when the teacher asked, "Is that clear to all?" Kenya students shot their hands up and said, "No, please explain more." It was not a traditional response and was often misinterpreted by both local students and teacher.

Another factor that required adjustment by both Kenya students and the college was the fact that the college had worked for several generations primarily with Nazarenes. These Kenya students were new to the Church and new as Christians. They had not grown up in a 50-year-old Nazarene congregation that had known and recommended them to be trained as church leaders. I was asking the college to serve not as a "finishing school" but as part of the "front line" evangelistic thrust. They would have to deal with eager but immature Christians who had voiced a call and shown potential. The college adjusted their stride remarkably. Two students were expelled for good reasons, and the message came across to all.

Four years later, the men came home changed. They had developed maturity and understanding. Shortly after his return, one of the men was appointed district superintendent of the area that includes Nairobi. This is an indication of the confidence and trust in the quality of training he received in Swaziland.

These methods of training were laying the groundwork for forming future Nazarene districts. In each area of Kenya, there would be several men who knew what the church was and could give stability to the new organization. We now added another pillar to the structure. On a very limited basis there would be the opportunity for qualifying men to do advanced work in one of our colleges in the States. I was open to this, although the cost was around $10,000 a year.

Certain types of training could not be obtained in any of our accessible schools in Africa. If we wanted Kenyans to teach in the new Africa Nazarene University, then they would have to obtain a master's degree from overseas. Dr. Leslie Parrott from Olivet Nazarene University rose to the occasion. He visited and talked with me in Kenya. Later, Mr. Lowell Malliet, the foreign student recruiter, came. As a result, there are a good number of Kenya students at Olivet today. One of them is a ministerial student from the Maasai tribe in Kenya, Paul Kisoso. He is a good student and has a sharp mind behind the tribal marks on his face. It has cost him the company of his family for several years. His wife and children often attend church in Nairobi, and from my office they talk by phone to that distant land, America.

I did not want an "elite" group coming back from Swaziland. There were many ways to be trained, and all were valid. To go to a far country was to gain tremendous respect and advantage automatically. I did not want a trip to Swaziland to become the only qualifying path for responsible office in the new church in East Africa.

The need to organize districts in Kenya before most of the highly trained men returned, helped to prevent this fear from becoming a reality. At the time of district organization, we recommended, and Dr. Jerald D. Johnson ordained, 20 older preachers in Kenya who had never had, and probably never would have, an opportunity to go away from home for an education. These factors dissipated all grounds for unhealthy leadership competition developing in this new work. "Not too fast but not too slow. Not too much but not too little." These phrases are vital in the pioneering of new work in the church.

The need to train large numbers of preachers here in Kenya led to the establishment of the Africa Nazarene University. The Kenya government gave full encouragement, and the plans started to gel. The purpose was an Africa seminary, and the way there lay in an income-generating university that would train at several levels.

Across Kenya and into Uganda during the first three years, the church had now grown into almost 150 congregations and pastors. By now there were many other types of ministry besides preaching. Several of these had come out of the involvement of Compassionate Ministries.

Nursery schools were becoming a regular part of many church programs. The seed money for this program came from Compassionate Ministries. Training centers for tailoring and carpentry were part of many of the church programs. When the church met the needs of a poor community by helping change the standard of living, it received a very favorable reaction from government and local people. These programs were all started with funds from Dr. Steve Weber's office in Kansas City. The teaching of simple skills helps our people attain self-support in their churches.

When I was a boy growing up in Africa, I was caught in a

fire in the bush once. It was a frightening experience. The long golden thatch grass stood six and seven feet high for miles. The heavy seed heads hung and swayed in the light breeze. I was working my way as quietly as possible upwind toward the river. In my hand was the small rifle that Dad had given me. I knew that at this late afternoon hour the reedbuck would be out along the river, and with any luck, I would get one for fresh meat for the mission station.

I had worked my way to within half a mile of the river when a slight change in the wind brought to my nose the faint but unmistakable smell of grass on fire.

I knew well the danger! Bushfire is awesome in its speed and intensity. I had seen it many times. Now I was instantly alert. I looked up, and for the first time I noticed that the sky above me was defused and hazy. Before I could start thinking, my legs started moving. I discarded all as I struggled to run through the matted, heavy grass and thornbush. I was constantly going from one side to the other dodging the trees and brush to get through.

As if the wind knew of my struggle, it, too, now joined the barriers that I faced. In 15 minutes, it was blowing strongly and gusting against my face. Smoke came with it in increasing density, carrying small black pieces of burned-out grass and dropping them on me. I could not turn back and run with the wind, as safety lay almost a mile away, and the fire would catch me long before I reached it. There was no safety in the trees, for the flames would leap higher than the highest of them. The only way out was a race against the oncoming flames to the river. If I could make the river before the fire, I might live. Otherwise, my only hope lay in finding an ant bear hole and getting into it regardless of what snake or hyena lived there.

At this time of the year, there would be only inches of water, but there was no choice. I was choking and my eyes burned. A warthog and several little ones fled past me, nearly bumping into me. They never turned as I leapt aside. Their tails were straight up and their heads held high as they followed the sow at high speed through the grass. Above me I saw storks and kites wheeling and diving toward the leading edge of the fire a mile away. I knew, as did they, that all the insect life and small animals would perish. The storks would walk for days through the black earth behind the fire and eat all the small mice and grasshoppers that they could find. The kites hung on the leading edge of the smoke and as the locust lifted into the wind, they were caught in sharp talons.

None of this mattered to me. I clutched my precious rifle, and tears of panic and frustration streaked the soot on my cheeks as I flung myself against the waving sea of brush higher than my head. I was close now and could sense the trees along the river more than see them. The gray smoke rolled down on me in dense waves, and the air was hot. I had found a game trail and blindly I followed it, knowing that it would lead to the river and life. It did, but just.

I could hear the flames ahead. At first a roar, faint but unmistakable, then distinct and continuous it bore down on me with breathtaking speed. The wind was now made by the heat of the fire and gusted strong and hard. The fire leapt a hundred yards at a time.

I wondered if some herdsman had set it in order to gain new grazing for his cattle. Or maybe it was someone trying to get at the bees in the trunk of one of the great baobab trees scattered about. Whatever started it, the entire bush was now a great wall of fire several miles wide and running ahead of a strong wind. Nothing would stop it until it ran into the mountains and rain came.

I stumbled down the bank and splashed into the few inches of water spread out over the sandbar. The precious gun was flung down and with both my hands locked together I scooped and scooped. The shallow water just covered me and kept me wet as long as I kept turning over and over. In seconds there was a great roar and the popping sounds of trees exploding. When the heat struck me I thought I was dying as I rolled over and over. The air seemed to be sucked from my lungs, and then the sound held and started to die. Finally, only the burning and popping in the reedbed was all that I could hear. The heat lessened. I opened my eyes, and the world had changed.

It was charred and black with trails of smoke from a thousand stubs of vegetation like so many obscene black candles. Flames flickered everywhere. The sandbar was black with smoking pieces of reeds, dried and ignited by the intensity of the heat. There was movement everywhere, and I jumped up searching for the gun. I knew that if any animal or snake had survived, it was only by doing what I had done and doing it in the same place as I.

Along the bank in the narrow but deeper water, there were dozens of cane rats swimming. They were harmless and as large as small dogs, and I did not fear them. Then across the sand, at the far side of the pool, flowed the snake. It was as thick as my arm, and it had been burned on part of its body. I watched only a second as it swept forward, paused, and swept forward again like a long shadow.

I waited no longer. Along the shallow riverbed I ran, splashing through the water and yelling to give myself courage. An hour later I came out at the bridge where the dirt road passed on its way to the trading post six miles away. I sat there on the side of the bridge for a long time and rested. On the other side of the road the grass was still long and brown and unburned. The wind had not blown that way.

Finally, a man with a bicycle came along and asked if I had been burned. When he was gone I took off all my clothes and washed them. I lay in the water until I, too, was clean before dressing and walking home as if nothing had happened, lest I be kept from going out alone next time. I spent an extra hour that night taking the gun apart and oiling it more carefully than usual while listening to Dad tell about the fire over on the river.

There have been several times these past five years when I would remember that boyhood experience and think of the rush and speed with which the church was leaping and growing, almost faster than we could follow and keep up with it. I am thankful that it is His church, and it is taught and guided by the Holy Spirit. But fire it is, and I am watching it with awe! But then, I serve a God who deals in fire.

5

Blowing Sand and Camels

There were always many of them, no matter how poor the village—always a welcome and feast of rejoicing for each newborn baby.

They could do no wrong. Endless patience and tolerance was shown them. Although loved and cuddled, a name was withheld a year or two just in case, like so many, they would not remain but be gone. Only the survivors had names.

Small sister, a year or two older, carried him on her back in play and tending. Life had not many free moments for mother, and time shared was shared from a warm skin or blanket tied tight around her back where the baby rode. Tears brought him around while she paused, and he sought the comfort of her attention and breast. Sheltered and carried close to her, he first learned of the world beyond her arms.

Whenever I entered a village, the children came flocking. Not too close at first. But close enough to watch and listen. As long as they were silent, African society let them sit and listen to any discussion the adults had. Lined against the wall in the deep shadows, they sat in silence, and except for tiny babies, they seldom made a move or sound. So they learned of life in this their classroom.

Sometimes a trickle of water spread out a few inches be-neath him, but usually it didn't matter as it soon disappeared into the hard earth floor. There was wisdom in not burdening each small child with clothes from the waist down. Fat, shiny stomach bulging, he stood on bowed legs and watched me, round eyes hardly meeting mine but seldom missing anything at all—always respectful, sometimes fearful.

It was only later, at age six and more, that he came close. He and his clan of tiny friends would laugh and giggle and play a game of push and see if you can touch him. The rules called for me not to notice, and usually I didn't. When they saw that I knew the rules, they grew bolder and shyly reached out to touch my pant leg or shoes as I sat talking to their parents in the hut.

But the prize above prizes was when I sat around the fire or they were in the seat behind me in the van. Then before long I would feel small hands so light as to be almost a shadow, touch my arm. An arm covered with dark coarse hair. Their fingers would run along it many times; it was simply fascinating.

But finally, when closeness and a movement or two permitted, they would touch the back of my head. So light at first that I could not be sure. But later when courage ran high, they would stroke my straight long hair in total amazement. Words played no role in this game, and in half a century in Africa I've played it so often that I know all the rules well and enjoy it thoroughly.

It's only much later, when age and friendship come hand in hand, that they will look up and gently touch white skin and say, "Does it hurt?" This is the age of laughter and smiles. There is no fear now. White teeth flashing and flying feet, clapping hands, and shouting in shrill unison, the children are the sound of joy in the African village.

This is why it was so wrong at Lodwar. There were 200 of them under the tree and not a smile and not a sound. Two hundred children and no shiny black skins, all were dull and dusty. Their stomachs stuck out, but something was wrong with the way it all looked. It was the legs and arms and faces that told the story. The legs and arms were knobby. The joints were the thick part, and there was no shape. They were just small, straight bones covered with skin and on top of them a huge stomach and small chest balanced, with each rib no bigger around than the bone of my finger, clearly visible to the eye.

The faces were shocking. They were solemn and old and sunken in. Cheekbones and deep eye sockets were the prominent features. An army of tiny soldiers stood before me. Their orders were to march to death, and they were not far from their fate. The giggles and laughter had died long ago when the corn and beans were gone. Their wise old eyes smiled no more, for a hundred times they had seen brother and playmate laid in the earth.

It was a new game now, a game played for keeps called "Don't Move." They did not move. And if they did, it was as if it were very cold. Maybe death by starving is cold. I do not know. I've never played that one. My conversation had always had trump words like "McDonalds" and "double thick." But I learn fast. And with 200 kids teaching me, it took only minutes. This memory will remain crystal clear until I stand in heaven.

Within months of our arriving in Kenya, Dr. Steve Weber contacted me and told me that there was a great, spontaneous response to the news of the famine in Ethiopia. We set dates, and both he and Dr. Richard Zanner flew in. Before they came, however, Beverly and I made three major trips up into northern Kenya. One of these took us to the border of Ethiopia. In the process, we found out that there was just as great a need on this side of the border as on the other. The famine stretched across all of north Africa.

With Dr. Weber came Mr. Rodney Adkins, one of the Compassionate Ministry field assistants. Following the planning session in Nairobi, we flew on into Ethiopia and scouted out the areas in which we felt the Church of the Nazarene could best help. Rodney and I traveled all over southern Ethiopia and spent a good deal of time in the camps.

I could not believe what I was part of. There were endless lines of shuffling people in rags that hung from skin and bone. Beside me stood the young American girl that was in charge of this camp with its tens of thousands of people. She had been drifting around Europe with a backpack and heard of the need so hitchhiked south into Africa. I had come north for the same purpose.

She was not yet 20 years old, but with the courage of youth, she was doing the impossible. "You look for the light. It's in the eyes," she told me. "If it's there, they will live. If it's not, then I place them on the left, and that group are all dead in a day or two. If it's there, they go right, and we try hard to save them. We still lose the babies though. They are hard to save, and there is almost always brain damage by now." I walked away thinking, "How do you decide who lives and who dies?" To the right and to the left.

Day after day we stood in the middle of death and watched the river of life flow past and over the brink into eternity. It was like standing in a dust storm and watching lives instead of dust swirl past and on. It never stopped, and there were few who survived. I did not ever become accustomed to it and could not lose my feeling for the individual person. I found myself talking to people and worrying about them as they sat in the lines. Would it be right or left?

Many times in my life I have been in situations where there was a split second to decide or there was instant death to follow. I've shot many, many lions and several at full charge. I had flown light planes in the mountains of Idaho and on the Kalahari of Africa. Things slow down in those split seconds, and I have no trouble thinking or reacting fast. But this situation was different. I simply could not be removed from it, and I could not detach myself from the problem.

Two weeks totally exhausted me both physically and emotionally. I saw the workers in the camps laughing and sitting talking, and it was always a shock to me. I watched one of the missionary pilots who flew into the camps daily, come and stand with his hands in his flight jacket and tell jokes. It was beyond my range of understanding.

My eyes would drop to a child lying on the blistering ground kicking away the last moment of his life. And I felt compelled to try and do something, knowing full well that it would not help. But detach myself, and tell jokes or laugh? Years later, I cannot tell or write of this without being overcome with emotion. Such is the battlefield that the Lord has placed us in.

One small child sat crying in the sun, and I bent over and reached down to pick him up. His head was huge for the size of his small body. Every vein stood out in stark relief on the dusty, dull black skin of his head and hands. He touched my closed hand and with a featherlike touch turned the open hand over. When he saw it was empty, his head dropped and he sobbed aloud. The moment was caught by Rodney Adkins from a distance away, by telephoto. He sent me a copy months later when it was printed in the church publications. Every time I see it, I can smell the dust and hear the child's weak cry.

In one of the camps, I stood and tried to gain control of my emotions and feelings. The sun was directly overhead. It was so hot that the trees seemed to float inches off the ground in the distance. There was a gray, waterlike haze on every horizon. Every object was distorted and stretched out. Some that were far seemed close, and others were upside down as if reflected. All shimmered and moved all the time. In the far distance, a caravan of camels was stretched out following one another slowly. They stood on long, thin legs that appeared twice the height of their bodies.

My ears rang with a high-pitched sound that was underlying all other sounds. There were other sounds. In fact there was a sea of both sight and sound that swept over and around me.

There were tens of thousands of pitiful remnants of humanity on all sides. The famine camp was packed with the living and the dead. I looked out from the edge of the huge tent where I stood and watched the old man coming toward the shade. He was not going to make it. There were no clothes on him except a dirty scrap of loincloth that failed to grant him any modesty. He was bent over and every rib stood out in clear shadow on the darkness of his skin. He never took a step without being bumped and pushed by the press of people moving slowly in every direction.

Hundreds of babies and children cried, and the sound of their voices were the curtain of sound that I heard. The old man had his left hand out in front of him now, and he never turned his head as he slowly took one step forward after another. His shuffle stopped, and he started to sway. Slowly, he toppled over and fell. No one paid the slightest attention, and he lay without any movement at all. He did not even roll over, and there was certainty in me that he was dead before he reached the ground.

I turned to the man near me who was giving out the packets of famine biscuits. I nodded toward the still form of the old man. The worker turned and shouted something. About 10 minutes later, two young men took a blanket and went over and rolled the body into it. Then, grasping the ends of the blanket, they carried him away, swaying in the blanket, to be placed with hundreds of others that did not make the shade. They would be buried at dusk in one large grave. No one moved aside or took notice as they passed. Twice they laid the burden down on the ground and stopped to talk to persons that they knew. Then they went around the side of the tent, and I lost sight of them.

Next to me at the table in the shade, the young social worker never paused in her work. The endless line of incoming people staggered past her. To each she gave a numbered card, and the man next to her directed the person to the section of the camp where they would live. The green tents, now weathered and billowing in the hot wind, stood in long rows into the distance. In one tent lay the babies. They were little more than thin piping cries. There were endless dark shadows around the edge of the work area. The mothers, hovering on the edge of death themselves, sat and held the barely living forms in their arms. No one departed, for the only hope lay in being right there all the time. The sobs of the mothers were a constant sound as they sat and watched the lives ebbing swiftly away.

In my briefcase was the first check for $50,000 to buy grain and place it in the camps. It came spontaneously out of the hearts of Nazarenes who had responded to the television reports of the famine. It would buy a week or month of new life. It would help them hold on until things changed and the rain came. It would wipe away the tears for some whose babies would not die and who would grow to manhood and someday maybe change the world that was so dry and full of sorrow. It would be done in the spirit of Christ who had told us to minister to the hungry and the cold and the fatherless.

Mr. Leo Mpoke, Kenya coordinator for Compassionate Ministries, traveled all over the northern part of Kenya and into both Ethiopia and Sudan. He sought out the worst areas and transported funds to insure that the food reached the people. I did not allow him to give it to an organization unless he personally had gone in and purchased the grain. This was done to insure that the financial integrity of a holiness denomination called the Church of the Nazarene would not be compromised. Every dime given was used in the famine. My salary and my travel were paid out of the General Budget and not from the famine funds. This is the way we are, and I am glad for it.

During this time, I was invited to appear at State House Nairobi and meet the president of Kenya. President Daniel Moi is a fine Christian leader, and when we met him and told him of the work of the Church of the Nazarene, we received a warm welcome. Beverly and the Mpoke family came with me. The entire meeting was carried live on television and reached every corner of the country. We were now known!

I still have a dream to bring a team to Kenya someday and build a church among the Turkana people of the north. We have people in our churches there who were won during the famine, and they need our help in His name. One of their pastors is studying in Nairobi to prepare for the ministry.

In the center of Northern Kenya there is a 50-square-mile volcanic mountain that rises up out of the low, hot bush. It is well-watered, and there are both men and elephants there.

Someday we will start a church there, too, and then another and another. During the height of the famine, we provided food for the people there. It is a ripe harvest field, and we are making plans to reach it.

6

Did Not Our Hearts Burn Within Us?

Very little ever challenged our African people like the quest for education. The footpaths in the rural areas were filled at dawn with children running to school. Many of them ran hours each way. The greatest tragedy was when, for lack of funds or some similar reason, a student dropped out and sat at home. The quest continued even when one was grown and married. Fathers and mothers were quite prepared to be separated for years if the opportunity arose to go overseas to study. In fact, the United States government would not grant a student visa readily if the family was not left behind as security that the student would return. Education would have to play a great role in the new work in Kenya.

Among the many things that required careful attention in the new work was the problem of preaching licenses. The men that I was reaching would have to have something, but there was one thing that worried me. There was hardly a day in Kenya when the press didn't print a story of some Christian minister in the country that had "jumped the rails." Without constant contact and teaching, I had no way of knowing the depth of spiritual life of our new men. The last thing we needed was adverse news coverage. We would be struck out before we came up to bat!

In the early days in Swaziland, my grandfather had faced a similar problem. I thought about his solution. It looked as if, with slight modification, it could work here too. He had started a quarterly meeting with workers and new Christians to talk out their problems. It was also a time of teaching and fellowship for them.

All contributed. He never bothered with preaching licenses. In fact, I do not recall the topic ever being written or spoken about until many years later when the structure of the organization became vast and men had to be appointed over others. The first ordination of nationals was in 1938, 25 years after the work had started. My father had been in that class. My grandfather was ordained in Africa by Dr. Reynolds on his first visit to Africa in 1914.

Instead of a local license—issued without any organized local church—I issued an identity card with a picture. It said only that the individual was identified with the church and needed to renew the card each year. This got the church off the hook until we knew what the man was like and gave us several years' time. It satisfied legal requirements.

At the General Assembly in Anaheim, Calif., I spent some time talking with the Gastineaus. When Dr. Zanner asked us if we would go into East Africa, I had asked him if it would be possible to get Roger and Rowena to come following their furlough. He had agreed to the move, and Roger and his family prepared to come. I was sure that they would provide us with talent in many areas of the work now developing. I was correct.

Roger and Rowena Gastineau helped me in both training and church work. Roger, with 15 years of experience in Zambia working with the national church, was particularly useful in the overall work. He had pioneered the concept of total self-support in the national church in Zambia. Subsidy was the traditional method that the Church of the Nazarene had used, and I doubt if any missionary would have thought that the church could survive without it. Roger put the concept of self-support into practice and sold it to the national church leaders there.

It has not only worked but become the policy of the entire region in Africa. In 1991, the final Nazarene churches on this continent will be paying their own way and giving generously for world evangelism. They, too, are concerned for the inner city of Chicago and Los Angeles. Roger's advice was on fertile soil in Kenya. I, too, had seen the demeaning and restrictive results of subsidy. Dr. Zanner and I had agreed that we would not start the process in the new work in Kenya. The only exceptions have been where we needed to place someone in the inner city to open work. There, for a limited time, we have helped cover the cost.

Rowena had developed a women's ministry now used not only by Nazarene missions but others as well. I thought of the training of the pastors and felt that she would fit into that perfectly. The bonus was that they had a family of four girls. They were Renatta, Robyn, Rene, and Rhian. Bev and I had just sent our last child off to America to college. We simply adopted their kids as our new family.

Roger was a golfer. I had never learned that game, because where I grew up, if you got that far from home, you had to carry a rifle. However, in good biblical fashion, I was a fisherman. I don't get to do it much, but I really enjoy it when I go. While Roger was new and still trying to get to know me, I took advantage of him and invited him and his family to come up to Lake Turkana for a day of fishing. I was eager to go, as I had read that there were perch in that lake that reached 300 pounds. They called them Nile perch.

I knew that if I ever caught one, it would be the fish story to beat all fish stories. Never again would I have to listen to pastors tell me about Alabama bass or Alaska salmon. Roger and his family came, and we took a day to drive up to this desolate lake, or more accurately, inland sea. It was several hundred miles long and 40 miles wide with several islands in it. There was only one lodge where we could stay, and it was hot.

Early in the morning, we took my little rubber boat down to the lake and pumped it up. We then strapped the 25-horse Johnson engine to it. With the help of some local Turkana men, we pushed it into the water and started trolling for Nile perch.

An hour or two in that heat and all of us had had enough. "We'll come back in the evening," I promised. Bev was seated on the floor in the front of the boat. I rode on one pontoon and held the tiller. Roger sat on the other pontoon facing me. We all started to reel in our lines. Bev's was first in, and she laid her rod and reel down in front of her in the boat. Mine was the next in, and I turned and started to lay it down. At that second the boat was struck by a tremendous impact that threw it into the air and brought it crashing down. I fell forward on my hands and knees and water cascaded down over me. Roger was half over me. As the water cleared and the boat rose and fell, throwing us around, Roger started yelling. One word was all I heard pitched so high I did not know where it came from. "Crocodile," he screamed, "crocodile." On hands and knees in the bottom of the boat, still gripping the tiller, I opened my eyes not a foot away from the sharp end of a 14-foot, one-ton, Nile crocodile.

He had lunged for us up on the boat and managed to get

the tapered end of the pontoon in his mouth. He thought he had someone and snapped his jaws shut. There were 12 holes right through that space-age "Hyperlon." Now he was trying to roll and dump us. I swung the engine against him and opened her up! Back and forth we swung. Then suddenly Roger grabbed my new little stout boat rod and Ocean City reel. He rose, and still yelling "Crocodile! Crocodile!" he swung the rod above his head and brought the reel down on top of the head of the crock. Blow after blow, and not even a tear in the eye of the crocodile!

The most exciting sound in the world has to be the sound of hissing air from a rubber boat in the middle of Lake Turkana, while locked in tooth-to-tooth combat with a crocodile!

The crocodile finally realized that he did not have one of us, and I saw his lips twitch as he made up his mind to lunge into the boat. If you don't think a crocodile has lips, you have never knelt four inches from his mouth and watched him. He had not counted on my vigilance. Roger was still pounding away. The reel was bent over on its side. The end plates were gone. The handle was gone. The star drag was gone. The rod was bent where it held the reel.

As the croc let go and started to lunge, I hit the throttle and the engine did everything the advertisement said it would do. We leapt forward, and we three missionaries, on our hands and knees, bounced over the water at 30 miles an hour, giving a rubber boat mouth-to-mouth resuscitation. We scooted up the sandbar at full throttle and bowled Turkana men over left and right. It must have taken us 50 yards to get stopped. I know it took Roger another 50 yards beyond that. I have not been able to get him to give up golf and go fishing with me again.

In the area of pastoral training, Rowena took over. She hammered out dozens of courses for the pastors' study program. She wrote to many of the other fields, including South America, and got their programs. From all this material she developed ours. It was a two-prong approach to training the pastors.

Later, both Roger and Rowena were given a special task in Work and Witness, and they are involved in that today.

At the close of the service at Nampa First Church in Idaho, a tall young man came up to me and introduced himself. "I'm Dan Anderson," he said. Dan Anderson—I had written and spoken the name many times, but this was our first meeting. The first time I had heard the name was when Dr. Zanner called from the States where he had just finished the interviews for new missionary candidates. "Harmon, I've got the perfect man for you. His name is Anderson, Dan and Melody Anderson. They come from around Sacramento and went to school at Nampa."

The Andersons had two small children, Becky and Danny. They, too, became our new grandchildren. I gave Danny a small fishing rod for Christmas one year. Some time later when I visited their home on the other side of Kenya, five-year-old Danny took me out and flicked the weight down the long drive between the rows of apartment buildings close by on either side. He was remarkable! I never did find out what it had cost Dan in broken windows for his son to reach that level of expertise.

The Gastineau family came nine months after we had opened the field. The Andersons arrived a little over a year after the field opened. For a long time they helped us make up the complete team.

Missionaries become a family. They work together for

years at a time. Their children grow up knowing other missionaries better than the relatives they left behind. After a lifetime on the field, the ties forged between missionaries are strong indeed. They have spent many, many hours side by side in lonely combat against the enemy.

While on furlough in 1989, I visited the campus of Point Loma for a speaking engagement. When chapel closed, there were several students who surged forward and ran up onto the platform. One after the other they threw their arms around me and then just hung on. They were missionary kids. The first to reach me was Renatta and after her were many others, some of whom I knew and some that I did not. It did not matter. I came from the field and that made me "family." Like a favorite uncle or someone sent by their fathers, I spent the rest of the morning in the cafeteria drinking coffee and listening to every detail of the new friends and the new life they were now entering. It is a very special "family" that one enters when you serve in the field, and it is a gift from God.

Many missionaries on furlough have stood in for parents on the other side of the world. Our eldest daughter, LeAnn, was now living in the States. We had flown to the field directors' meeting at the regional offices when I received an emergency message. LeAnn was in the intensive care unit of a hospital in Oklahoma City. She was critical and on life-support systems. They were not sure what the trouble was. We knew that she had not been well for some time and that they had run quite a number of tests.

Within hours, the results were back. It was Hodgkins disease. Cancer! Her neck had swollen and her breathing was affected, but the team had been called in and they had started an immediate treatment with a menu of chemo drugs. It took a year, and Nazarenes contacted us from everywhere with assurance of prayer. God touched her, and she is up and about, showing no sign of cancer. I couldn't be there for her illness or the wedding that followed her recovery. "Thanks, Walt Crow, for standing in for me. I'm told that it was a beautiful wedding."

During Dan's third year on the field, he gave us all some concern. They were living at Kisumu on Lake Victoria. It was low and hot country. With that much water, there was a good deal of malaria, and both Dan and Danny came down with it. Father and son were up in a week. However, the next time it was not that simple. Dan came down and did not respond to the treatment with Fanzidar. It was not until Melody had rushed him to a hospital and tests had been made that we found out that it was both malaria and typhoid together. Bev and I immediately drove across Kenya to help Melody. For a week we prayed and Dan fought. In time, the Lord answered prayer, and he rallied and recovered. Then we went home again. When little Danny was so ill, I was as concerned as if it had been my own child. These children are part of the gift of love that the Lord gives us so far from our own family.

Dr. Johnson and Dr. Zanner flew in for a couple days, and I flew them over to the Sunday dedication of the Homa-Bay Church. Chattanooga First Church had sent a team, and they had just finished building. There were around 1,200 people there for the service in the new church. A few months later, Dr. Scott flew in. Again we flew him to the other side of Kenya, and Dan met us at the airstrip. He drove us to the church 10 miles away for the morning service. There were 1,600 people gathered, and the church could hold less than 500. I watched Dr. Scott wipe tears from his eyes as he looked out over these new Nazarenes.

These were busy days with the work spreading out ever

further. There never was enough time to finish what lay on the desk in the office. In trying to keep pace with it all, I found myself facing things that I had never in my entire life faced. For the first time I learned what stress can do.

God gave me a very high energy level, and stress had not bothered me. Not until I started staying awake at night and then started having trouble with muscle cramps all the time. The cramps were so severe that they prevented me from getting into the car or stepping on the brakes or climbing the stairs at home. Finally, every muscle in my body started twitching and would not stop. I've had muscle twitches before, but not like this. Even on my scalp under my hair they twitched. My doctor warned me to back off, but I could not. There were less than half the hours I needed. The phone rang all day from Kenya and all night from the U.S.A. It was day in America when it was night here, and we were on direct dial.

Occasionally there was total panic. I remember well the day when one of the Work and Witness teams of 16 people arrived a day early. That was all right except it was 22 hours until the outgoing team boarded the flight home. We had no extra rooms for the jet-lagged people and could not strip beds and do the laundry for the incoming group. There was food to be cooked and chairs for all. Fortunately all pitched in and were good sports about it, and we made it. The days were full however. Bev and Rowena did the washing of the sheets while the outgoing team helped.

During the visit to the doctor he told me to take time off and get away, but I could not. So he said, "Well, I'll give you a vacation at home then. Take one of these morning and night for a week." I took one that night not knowing what it was. In the morning the sun never came up for me. I remember at around ten o'clock going down the street in Nairobi with Roger on one side and Beverly on the other trying to get to the lawyer's office to sign documents on something. They were laughing, and I was in another world. I never took the second pill, but it took all that day to recover.

At the beginning of 1989 Dr. Zanner came in, and I asked him to appoint Dan as mission director. That lifted part of the load. The responsibility for the care of the growing group of missionaries now fell on him. He did a superb job.

In mid 1990 Dr. Zanner has promised to help me get a full-time office manager and finance control person. That will lift all but the administrative work and the opening of the new work in Rwanda, Zaire, and Uganda. There will also remain the office plus the legal work over it all, but that is manageable.

The forming of new districts was especially helpful. Almost every church needed help in gaining land on which to build. They sought many ways to finance this, and they needed letters from my office to carry to the endless levels of government. In African society, one never approaches the need or question directly. So, much of my time is spent waiting for the point to be made. I have tried everything. A man will not tell a woman anything about business, so my secretary is of limited help. We printed forms to be filled out by persons seeking an appointment. That did not work.

When Dr. Johnson came in early 1989, we talked about the church growth and decided to move ahead with the forming of a district with a national superintendent. That would help a great deal, as he would care for the churches and I would handle only those needs that he referred to me. As we looked at the numbers and the layout of the country, however, it became clear that one man could not do this. Finally, Dr. Johnson and Dr. Zanner approved the forming of four districts. This took place in Nairobi on January 27, 1990.

As I faced this reorganization, I spent a lot of time during the year carefully feeling out the preachers and missionaries to enable me to make a recommendation concerning both the new leaders and the district officers. It would involve taking a great step of faith because of the short time the work had been here. But if we did not do it, there would be no way I could continue to supervise it all, and growth would stop. When that happens, the work sometimes starts backward. The rebuilding is always more difficult.

The district superintendents are fine men and well-respected leaders. They had served with me in the work long enough that they had adopted the set of principles that I used. For instance, in taking people into the church, I had not thrown it open to a group or congregation to just transfer in. We had insisted that every person come in on his own. In this manner, we had avoided the problem of a preacher that was coming in, later taking all his people out again with him if he left.

Most of the preachers had a background in some other denomination. We very carefully covered their views when we were working with them on joining our church. Seldom did we lose anyone as a result. One of these new district superintendents had an interesting conversation with me a few weeks after he was appointed. It seems that there was a problem surrounding the selection of a leader in one of our sister denominations. This young man had come from that denomination several years back. He proceeded to caution me not to respond to the many applications that the church was receiving as a result of the problem. "I am afraid they will divide us at a later date," he said. I have been glad many times for the insight and developing loyalty of these new Nazarenes.

7

The Tools of Leadership

Out at the edge of Nairobi, not far from the Ngong Hills, there was a beautiful piece of land. It was like Eden must have been. There were great flat-topped thorn trees with giraffes standing under them. Herds of zebra and impala were scattered across the rolling hills. Beverly and I stood and looked, and then we started to pace it off. Along one side there was a deep and a beautiful canyon with ledges and cliffs. At last we were back where we had started. The Lord told me clearly that this was holy ground, and we stood with heads bowed and by faith dedicated it to His service.

In my heart there was both deep concern and a great hope. I knew, having lived all my life in Africa, that the church was facing critical times. In some parts of Africa we were now teaching our third generation of Nazarene national children in our own schools. Many of our African people had gone on beyond what we offered and had become very successful in their areas of work. There were Nazarene laymen in business who could afford to fly anywhere in the world and had the best imported cars. They were involved in the financing and building of their own churches. Many were in government at the highest levels. Several were now doctors.

At the time I went to Kenya, in all parts of Africa, there were less than a dozen ordained preachers who had high school diplomas, and only a couple had college degrees. Bible schools were great, but they often had to gear the program toward students with very little formal education. They offered limited training when it came to leadership. They taught the Course of Study for the ministry, sometimes with very limited resources and under great difficulties. What we needed and wanted for Africa was much more. I had the feeling that much of the strength of the American church lay in the fact that from the beginning of its history we had good colleges to train our youth. These included good training for those who were going into the ministry and for generations of great and strong laymen.

The Church of the Nazarene International was now demanding that the church on the mission field take over their own support and assume responsibility for their part of the world. But as a denomination, we had failed to give African churches the tools of leadership. We had not planned for the fact that someday Africa would change. It would not always be smoke-filled huts and people who could not read or write. Someday the church would face laymen who controlled the destiny of the richest continent in the world.

As Africa, the mighty giant, was now awakening, we would have to offer the church the same weapons that we had used in the mother church, or we would soon lose the most talented people of the African church. Without educated ministers, who would preach to the educated laymen that we already had? The people outside of Africa often viewed Africans as "herdsmen" and "forest dwellers." We had those, but we also had a fast growing number of technical and professional men and women. In Nairobi, there were Ph.D.'s in the Central Church congregation. Where was I to find a pastor who could relate to the demands of these gifted people that God had given us?

I had lived in Africa and had been part of the scene since

missionaries rode horses. I had watched the work expand into every country of South and Central America and much of the rest of the world. We were still largely confined to southern Africa. Now, South Africa looked like it would spend years in flames and turmoil.

Never had there been a more difficult time. In the States, the stockmarket had just crashed. Although this often bypassed the church people who gave funds, the scare perpetuated by the constant media reports and analyses led to fear, and fear led to a withdrawal from any venture that would cost anything.

When the Africa field directors met with Dr. Zanner and Dr. Strickland, the word was "GO!" Dr. Zanner went to the General Board with the unanimous recommendation of all of us and the promise of support from Dr. Strickland. We started to pray across the work, and I got on the phone and called a vast number of friends in America to join me in prayer. By the time Dr. Zanner presented the project, $248,000 in cash and pledges had come in to establish a seminary. Within days of the return of Dr. Zanner, I received a copy of the following letter:

Dear Dr. Scott,

> This is to confirm my report to you that the Board of General Superintendents has approved the U-level plan for ministerial education in Kenya with the plan to move to G-level as soon as feasible and in harmony with the recommendation of the Education Commission. We are most grateful for the gifts that have been provided for this, and we trust that it will continue to be a great project of interest to our people. I feel that it is a wonderful move for the continent of Africa and for the entire mission work across that area.
>
> *Sincerely,*
> CHARLES H. STRICKLAND

Ted Esselstyn and I had grown up together. There were no schools for me to attend when I was a child, and my parents sent me to live with the Esselstyns in the city. Ted and I shared his bedroom for several years and grew to know and respect each other as brothers.

He was always the top student and detail man. I was the dreamer and the darer. I fought the kids that taunted or bullied him, and although he was a year behind me, he checked my homework. I'm afraid I often got him into trouble with his parents. There were deserted and forbidden mine shafts to explore and dams and rivers to swim. I remember the day I came home with four revolver bullets and talked him into climbing up onto the garage wall and dropping bricks onto them. The police, drawn by the sound of shots, never found us down behind the water tank, but Ted's dad did!

As missionaries, we had often shared the need to train the preachers. He had served as the head of the Lula Schmelzenbach Bible College, and I was involved in sending a great number of student pastors there. He and I understood the system. We also understood the fact that most things come about by faith and going ahead and doing it. Both of us felt the need for getting on with the training of African ministers to our denominational standards. This feeling was also shared by many others in Africa. In Kenya, the Lord was now giving us the platform from which to work. He also opened the door to me for some finance to see it started.

Ted provided the solid thought and years of advanced educational training to put it together in working form. Twice in the early stages, he turned out a softcover book overnight with complete outline and plans for the project we dreamed of. He knew, from years of work, what the average costs would be in a Bible college and could give good projections. He was a good member of the team! It started with the Lord forcing us to do something. Many of the new pastors and evangelists in Kenya had not grown up in the Church of the Nazarene and had no real deep loyalty to our organization. They could get no training to make them Nazarenes, as there was no school close enough. This fact would also bear on their ordination and their conduct and understanding of our ethics. There was no way to supervise that many new churches and pastors. So it was imperative that we work out a system to train the men and teach them who we were.

It started with the search for land. It took some time for me to discover that as long as there was no special fund set aside for this, I would not get the green light on any land. Option after option ran out, and both owners and estate agents began to wonder what would be needed.

One ideal piece opened up just inside the city limits. It was half a mile from the United Nations headquarters for Africa and across the paved road from an embassy suburb. Again, the official answer was "wait awhile."

At this point, I inquired about what was needed to gain approval and discovered that the problem was funding. That led to the involvement of a legion of angels and the beginning of an exciting ministry in lay participation on the mission field.

Some time before this, I had been in the United States for a speaking engagement at Detroit First Church. As the message came to a close, a young man stood to his feet and asked how he personally could help on the field. Rich's question opened the first chapter of one of the most remarkable ministries I have been associated with. At that time, I was engaged in raising funds to help open the work in the country of Botswana. His participation led to his going to Botswana and giving the funds for the four-wheel-drive vehicle that would be needed there.

During the next five years, he and his wife became close and trusted friends of Beverly and me. They spent many weeks in Africa and were among the first to come to Kenya to be with us.

As we found the Lord's will for the seminary, Richard became deeply committed to it. He ran no great factory. But all that he had was committed to the Lord, and he handed over all the "loaves and fishes" that the Lord had given him. He had the privilege of watching the miracle unfold.

Richard and I both felt that the entire project should be cash. The mission field is not able to invest or generate funds at field level. We operate on a zero balance budget. Richard and Grace gave to help start it and purchase the land. Others, together with some of the churches, made up the balance. God had again answered prayer, and we were off and running.

In the next four years, this faithful couple would pledge and raise the funds to open Rwanda. There was no need to draw from General Budget for opening that great country or for the Africa seminary. They pledged and supplied the funds for the startup of classes and the multitude of costs that were unexpected. A year later they would again step forward and give to finish four of the buildings and let us get on with the rest of phase one so that the students and Work and Witness teams could live on the site and be comfortable and safe.

Two people, a husband and wife, were faithful with what God put into their hands and consequently were blessed and blessed again as they saw the multitude fed through their faith. It still goes on today. They are part of the legion of angels that God has used in opening East Africa.

Then there was Don, who came in and took a drawing

board and started to draw plans. He continued to come out to Africa two or more times a year and measure and draw. He paid his own way. From his hands came the master plan and the buildings. He mobilized other Christian architects. The pencil lines became concrete and bricks, and the bricks became buildings filled with young men and women praising the Lord.

Don and his wife, Lee, became part of our family out here. Like Moses, God simply asked him, "What is that in thy hand?" He found that even a pencil, touched by the Master, became priceless in the building of the Kingdom.

Don and Lee shared another miracle with us. This one was personal. One of the good reasons I have for hanging around when the Master is breaking the loaves and handing out the fish is that some of it ends up in my mouth too. However, I never expected what happened next.

Just before leaving for the States in 1989 for a three-month furlough, I received a letter from an old friend down in Alabama. "Harmon, bring Bev and come by while you are here. I want to talk to you." Out of that lunch with Don, Lee, Chester, and Margaret came the answers to one of the greatest concerns that any missionary has. Chester had made arrangements with Don to secure an apartment in Nashville at Old Hickory next to the Nazarene church where we could retire some day. The rent would pay off the balance owing. Don would oversee it until we needed it. Since my family has lived in Africa most of this century, there were few resources or options left in America. We simply did not know how to thank either the Master or the steward adequately for such care and love given from His hand to us.

In 1958, I had graduated from Nampa, a year ahead of Bev. We had attended classes with one who stepped forward to help change this continent for God. Bob and his wife, Yvonne, had met Mark and Clarice Moore. They decided to come out on one of the first Work and Witness teams. Bob has the gift of good organization, and Yvonne has boundless energy and access to the correct technical aid to put it together.

What has come from their involvement is phenomenal. They put together several special teams a year and bring them to Kenya. They round up the professionals, and when we run into trouble in the building program, out they come. Often Bob has picked up the cost himself. They set up a toll-free number in the States, and as I traveled, I simply referred people to that number. Yvonne knows the correct answers to their questions and helps find the cheapest fares to Africa.

On the field, Bob looked over the setup we had. He realized we would need to have housing for the teachers and for the teams if our plan was to work. He contacted an Asian who was short on sufficient funds to complete the building of a block of apartments. We were granted the use of six very nice apartments for several years for our visiting professors. And the man completed his building.

Close to where the Gastineau family lives, Roger found a large house and several apartments that were one property. He arranged with the owner to renovate and rent it for the visiting teams. It was one block walking distance to the Gastineaus' home and totally self-contained. There were plenty of hot showers and a large lounge for the evenings.

Our regular Work and Witness program places missionaries representing different aspects of the work with the team while they are here. We try to give them the widest possible exposure during the two weeks they spend in Africa. Through the help and vision of Bob and Yvonne, this has become possible. It was Bob who came one night and told me that my father had gone to heaven. He is a brother to me, and she is a sister. Together we are trying to win Africa.

There have been so many others. Disciples and followers who have jumped forward to help with talent and finance. Rex, from Washington state, saw us struggling to transport people to the building site in our cars and vans. He gave the funds for a bus. The teams can now be driven out to the site by one missionary.

There was Pat and Sue, who came and worked on a church. They had never seen blocks made in several different sizes of wooden molds. It was not possible to build and make it look beautiful or even strong. When they went home, she gave up new carpeting, and they borrowed against their house. Their district also helped, and the next thing I knew there was a high-speed block-making machine on the dock in Mombasa for us. Pat is a great fisherman, and I arranged to have him taken out to Lake Victoria on his next trip. He landed half-a-dozen huge, 35-lb., Nile perch. Fishers of men, all with the right priorities and the willingness to cast the net.

Several people sent memorials in honor of loved ones. These have gone into the college or the Central Nairobi Church. Norman remembered his wife in this way. At Central Church, a 400-capacity hall has been built that is serving as a sanctuary. It was in that hall that we met for a special occasion. Everything still smelled of varnish, and the glass still had fresh smudges from new putty. Dr. Jerald D. Johnson called four men forward and appointed them to be the first Kenyan district superintendents. The next day he ordained the first 20 Nazarene ministers on the east side of Africa. We have truly dedicated that gift and blessed that memorial! Other names of the great warriors are recalled every time I open a book on the shelves of a holiness college library. Among the names are those of Strickland and Ralph Earle.

How does one respond to a living gift to the Kingdom? After the General Board had given the green light on the seminary and the land had been selected and purchased, Dr. Zanner called Dr. Esselstyn and me together for a critical meeting. We needed a man; God's man for this hour in Africa. It had to be someone with special skill and talent—someone with knowledge and ability and a far horizon for a vision. It must be a person with a wealth of experience. The person would have to be strong and mature and not bothered by cultural change. The list went on and on. It ended with the statement that this person could not cost anything as there were no funds to pay them.

The requirements were many, and the list of possible people grew shorter and shorter. At last there was born in our minds an idea. We knew the man, but would he do it? He had every qualification, but he had recently retired. Then Dr. Esselstyn spoke up, "That is in our favor. The man will never stop, and if he feels God is challenging him to it, he will see it through." On that remark we voted unanimously to ask Dr. and Mrs. Mark Moore to come to Kenya and put together the organization of the seminary.

The way Mark tells it, they were just sitting down to breakfast in their retirement house when the phone rang. It was Dr. Esselstyn calling from Africa, and Mark covered the mouthpiece and whispered to Clarice who it was. I don't know how many years it takes to get really good at intuition, but I understand that at about that point Clarice started folding curtains and taking down pictures. What an adventure her life has been! The World Mission Division issued them a specialized assignment contract for three years.

Dr. Moore had been the district superintendent in Illinois. Then he had taken on the tremendous task of the presidency of Trevecca Nazarene College. In later years he had served as the denominational director of education for our colleges and universities. Along with these positions, he had served on the General Board for many years and in many capacities. In fact, he had served on the World Mission Committee in the General Board and had helped to forge the policies.

Mark and Clarice arrived in late spring of 1988. Not long after that, their 40-foot container arrived with their personal goods plus a houseful of furniture and a 40-kva generator for the seminary. Everything was carefully removed and the container positioned with the generator at the back against the doors. It was too large and heavy to transport alone. We hooked the winch on my station wagon to it and down it came ever so slowly. When the end was on the ground, we just drove the truck away and dropped the other end of the container to the ground.

Mark threw himself into the work of determining what the Kenya government wanted in education in order for us to have an accredited seminary. He found that they considered it a university and the requirements were the same. We already knew from seminaries in other parts of the world that they cost General Budget money to operate and train for ministry. A university offered a wider number of faculties than a seminary. At that time, the existing universities in Kenya were able to take in only about 6 percent of the eligible students. Ninety-four percent would pay their way through university for an education. There might be a way to save the denomination a great deal of money and also meet the needs of our laymen with good Christian schooling.

Many years back a young Methodist couple from Kenya had come to Olivet Nazarene College. They started work on their degrees. They were John and Leah Marangu. Today they both have earned Ph.D.'s and full professorships. They live in Kenya, and each has charge of a department in one of the universities. They are members of Nairobi Central Church, and John is a member of the District Advisory Board. From the second year I was here, Dr. Esselstyn and I had been working with the Marangus in determining the way our ministry in education would follow.

Both of these fine committed Nazarenes were involved in higher education in Kenya, and they knew all the pitfalls and requirements. In fact, we were unable to use Leah on our board because it would create a conflict of interest in regard to her work on the Government Commission for Higher Education. However, Professor John Marangu is a member of the "Trustees." Without their close guidance and practical involvement, I wonder if it would have been possible to carry out this great endeavor at all. Certainly it would have taken much longer and been much more difficult. In a situation where it is very important "who" you know as well as what you know, they know everyone. Dr. John Marangu dedicated himself to removing obstacles.

John had served on the Olivet faculty for several years and knew Dr. Leslie Parrott well. Dr. Parrott was flown to Kenya by Olivet and served on the Advisory Committee that was set up to get things rolling. His steady hand and wise counsel were a great help during this time.

It is a long road, and in the interim, we are not permitted by the government to refer to the institution except with the word *Proposed* before the title "Africa Nazarene University."

There are to be three institutions of training. These are:

1. The Graduate Seminary (G level). In the future this seminary is to offer the M.A. degree and be for all of Africa.

2. The Bachelors Seminary (U level). This institution will offer the Th.B. degree. It will serve primarily East Africa ministerial students.

These two are one school offering two accredited degrees.

3. The Kenya Nazarene Bible College (A level). Here studies are offered to ministerial students at the secondary education level. It meets the needs of less-educated candidates working toward ordination.

4. Institute for Human Resource Development. Training for ministers in bivocational skills to prepare them for community service and self-support.

In August 1989 Dr. Moore presented the "Proposal" to establish the Africa Nazarene University to the secretariat of the Commission for Higher Education in Kenya.

On January 26, 1990, during Dr. Jerald D. Johnson's visit to Kenya, eight of us met at the Nairobi Hilton, and seven of us formed the "Africa Nazarene Educational Trust." We signed the legal documents and became the Board of Trustees. I looked across the table and there was a smile on Ted's face as he glanced back at me.

8

The Men with the Spears

If the writer of the Book of Hebrews were alive today, I feel that the Lord would direct him to include in the 11th chapter on faith a vast host of modern African apostles. I think it might read something like this:

> And what more shall I say? I do not have time to tell about Alfred, Wycliff, Joseph, Souspeter, Julius, Johnson, Charles, and the other prophets, who through faith conquered kingdoms, as Stephen did in Uganda, administered justice as Benjamin did before the law of the land, and gained freedom of registration and what was promised; who shut the mouths of lions along the footpaths in the bush country of Tanzania for Joseph and Charleston. Quenched the fury of flames, and escaped the edge of Idi Amin's sword; whose weakness and lack of education was turned to strength; and who became powerful in preaching before presidents and kings. Women received back their dead raised to life again from malaria, cholera, and typhoid. Others were tortured and refused to be released, so that they might gain a better resurrection. They dwelt in poverty and hunger, they were flogged and jeered. They went about in sheepskins and goatskins, destitute, persecuted, and mistreated. The world was not worthy of them. They wandered in the deserts and mountains and in the caves of Africa. But all kept the faith unto the end.

Without the men touched of God, all would be lost. Balance was everything. Too much too fast and it would get out of control. Too little too slow and it would wither and die. In those first three years, I felt like a swimmer. The power of a rising ocean wave rushes forward, and your feet no longer hold you as the water lifts and pushes with a force you cannot counter. You are lifted up. Every effort is in keeping your head up and facing the direction you are traveling. When at last the wave is spent and feet are once more on sand, there is a sigh of relief and you tell yourself that there was no fear, you were in control all along. But deep inside you know that there was little you could do to control the great force that lifted you and moved you many yards forward.

The growth of the church across East Africa was like that. In the beginning, the preaching points were just places and people. In time they became familiar people and places that we learned to know personally. Approximately 140 congregations were started. Then I stopped opening new places. There were so many men wanting to preach that we lost track and printed applications and set up files. Rowena and Leo's wife, Francene, both worked to put together what became "The Office."

A center in Nairobi was paramount to the identity and stability of the work. It was necessary to build a large, visible church in the downtown area where we could hold assemblies and conferences. It would serve to establish our presence in a land where we were not well-known. It had to say we were there to stay. It was needed to serve as the center of our work across East Africa, not only the country of Kenya.

The first pastor should be a key man in many special ways. Because the church was both urban and central, the pastor should be nontribal if possible. He must be ordained and experienced in organization. He must know how to construct the needed buildings and would have to live on little salary. He would need both evangelistic and pastoral talent in abundance in order to reach key people. His wife would be part of all this and would become a key part of his ministry too. The regional office granted us $300 a month for two years toward the cost of this pastor. They also gave us an Alabaster allocation of $30,000 toward the building of the church and the two-story annex that would also serve as a preschool.

Rev. and Mrs. David Holmes felt the Lord leading them in this great task. David had been a licensed engineer prior to entering the ministry. He had worked in the ship building industry in England before becoming a Christian. Now he was an experienced pastor with an excellent record in both pastoring and the building of church buildings. During the three years that followed their arrival, the church grew until it could hold no more in the temporary chapel. Often the piano was carried outside, and the congregation met in the sun on the slab as parts of the new unit rose around them.

Three years later, the month before Dave and Jan left, they were able to move into the new fellowship hall. It seats 400, and it will not be long until the main sanctuary must be completed. The entire new unit has been done with Work and Witness teams and local workmen. It is made of square cut rock, and each rock is brought to the site and cut by hand with a hammer and chisel. Three old men do it all. The field center in Nairobi was built around the old building that was on the land and the new church complex that is rising today. It was very visible along one of Nairobi's main highways.

Before coming to Kenya, I had arranged for several teams of Work and Witness people to come to Africa. We called on these same teams to help us in Kenya. The first two teams worked on the old field center building, and they lived with

Bev and me, sleeping on cots and the floor. They were a real blessing. Several more teams followed, and we started to build churches in western Kenya. They stayed in the Andersons' home and drove out each day to the work site. In this way our ministry was multiplied many times over.

Soon all of the missionaries had a special part to play, and we all pitched in and helped each other in times of need. I had shared with each of them my feeling that the work was a team effort. We were not here to build our own empire but to put everything into the building of His kingdom. On the church building site we often had 100 local people joining in. Many spoke English, and the team members were often invited into schools and homes to visit and speak. Over the years, many team members have come back again, and several have come back three and four times.

People started to realize that Africa was not too far away for teams to come and work. It also proved that the cost was within reach if we kept it on the field. To do this, we sought ways to house the teams ourselves.

We knew that Africa was still the only place in the world where you could get up in the morning and see an elephant 50 feet away in the dawn light. Kenya, with its abundant game parks, was the best place in all Africa to see that. We decided that in the limited time of a team's visit we would try and give them education, inspiration, and fun that would help them remember and promote missions and the work in Kenya.

Roger and Rowena Gastineau were assigned to host all the Work and Witness teams coming into Kenya. This was the major part of their full-time assignment on the field. It required them to meet the teams at the airport and to see them off. Most jumbo jets arrive and depart around midnight, so they spent many long nights waiting for delayed flights.

Work and Witness Director David Hayse flew in from Kansas City. After a good deal of discussion we decided that two weeks would be the maximum time a team should stay and work. This would allow the missionaries to get their other tasks done. While a team was here, much of the missionaries' time was taken.

We could handle 16 people in the rooms that we had, so the teams were limited to that number. We could still do the buying and repair work on equipment and vehicles if we had at least one week between teams. So, we made that part of our policy. Then, to allow the people to get the most out of their visit to Africa, we planned for them to arrive on Friday, and rest and shop the next day. This gem of wisdom came from the experience of watching one eager carpenter cut through the electric cord twice in one morning due to jet lag.

The first Sunday we took them all out into a small starting church. This gave the team members an opportunity to see how mission work starts. The following Sunday we took them to Nairobi Central Church, which was just the opposite. The church was all but self-supporting and had everything well organized and much like they knew at home. They came away with a wide view of the variety in mission work.

On the second weekend following the Sunday morning service, we planned to take them down into the Serengeti. This was Africa's richest game area. It is live "Wild Kingdom." We drew up a contract with a mid-priced tented camp and also with a tour company for four minibuses and drivers. This covered us for insurance and gave the people a professional tour of one of the world's greatest attractions.

The Work and Witness program has proven to be one of the greatest blessings possible to our work in Kenya. Hundreds of laymen have come and worked here, and there is an ongoing list of people who have made arrangements to come in the future. This has made possible the building of the entire college campus at no cost to the General Budget. These teams have taught our own people something about the spirit of service. They have, in fact, multiplied our hands and feet as missionaries.

Every missionary has a particular assignment to fill. We work around the personal needs of each family. For instance, Melody Anderson had her hands full with a young family. We asked her to take the job of making a written schedule for the missionaries and then seeing to it that the church publications were always aware of what was going on here. She has done a superb job, and Kenya is today a household word in the denomination.

Dan Anderson, her husband, was asked to supervise the church across western Kenya. This covered about two-thirds of the churches in Kenya. As the pastors were so new to the ways of the Church of the Nazarene, this was a difficult job. Dan later helped with the extension teaching. All the work in that part of the field fell on him, including the building program. The Andersons kept several groups of Work and Witness teams in their home for weeks at a time while the teams built churches.

The Lord smiled on us in a special way when he sent us Dan. He had worked in a bank and could keep books. Few people can keep the level of books that are needed on a mission field such as this one. He talked the bank into doing many things for the church that we did not even know could be done. A $50,000 line of instant credit was one of the more useful items! His books for the council are always balanced and done by computer printout.

At the beginning of Dan's fourth year, I requested that he

be appointed the mission director for the Kenya Council. The regional office and the World Mission Division granted my request.

Al and Kitty Jones of San Jose, Calif., came in February of 1990. Al was placed in charge of developing and implementing an extension teaching program for the college. There were many men with large families and established churches. They could not pull up roots and come in to the college for years at a time. Al was asked to reach and teach these men as part of his work. This requires a lot of infield work. They moved into the upstairs apartment in the Field Center where they would be available to the district superintendents and started working.

The wives on the field serve in vital and assigned work. Very little of their time is spent serving tea! Missionary wives are paid a salary equal to that of the husband. Every wife on the Kenya field earns it. Mark made his wife, Clarice, the dean of the new college. She had spent years in colleges and knew the job and also knew how to get people to help her. Clarice has laid the foundation for a program that will not need adjusting in the years ahead.

Beverly was appointed as bookkeeper and interim treasurer for the field since the Andersons were on furlough. Normally, the wife of the field director does not serve in this capacity. But until a missionary is assigned to devote full-time to it, Beverly stands in. It was not new to her. Over the years she had served as the treasurer in several fields and councils. She, too, always hands me a computer printout on time!

Another factor that affects each family is the ongoing correspondence with the church in other parts of the world. If the church anywhere in the world is contacted about a matter relating to East Africa, that mail comes to my desk. Our mail includes all the government mail from several countries and the typing and filing that goes with it. Mixed into this somewhere is time for visits with many new pastors and laymen who drop by to talk. In keeping with the courtesy of the traditions of old Africa, it would be impolite to be too hasty.

Long ago the missionary moved into the space age in a literal sense. He had always tried to be there in a spiritual sense. We were needing to contact the regional office and Kansas City all the time regarding permission, guidance, policy, and the transfer of funds. They did not teach computer science 35 years ago at NNC. However, my office today has two computers given to us by laymen in the church. As I constantly fly from country to country and visit churches and leaders, I carry a laptop computer containing a vast memory and a hard disk. It gets plugged in back at the office, and all my ongoing work remains behind when I leave. We were able to get only one phone line to my work office in Nairobi. So, at 6 P.M., that phone line switches to the fax and the messages from the regional office start printing out. Then those from Kansas City come in. We are usually able to answer back and forth in a few seconds. I'm trying to make a modem work too, so that entire files can be sent in seconds. I haven't managed to get the different types of phone lines to cooperate yet, but I will in time. It's a different age today!

As we look back on the past five years, we rejoice at the advances, but we are also concerned by the defeats. Much of the area that I am responsible for is inaccessible from the ground. There have been wars leaving tens of thousands of automatic weapons in the hands of sometimes starving people in a world where there is often little or no rule of law. When the gun kills, no organization follows up to find out who did it. Kenya has largely overcome this problem, but in some of the surrounding countries, there are areas where it would be suicidal to travel. Yet, there are people there in vast numbers, and now there are Nazarene churches.

Some time ago, I was able to get back to the States, and I sat a long while visiting with my father. He had lost 40 pounds in his battle with cancer, but his eyes were bright as he listened. I told him about snow on the equator and a lake that stretched so far it took an hour to cross it in a plane. We talked about how it felt to walk in the still-deep shadow under the rain forest beside a pygmy. I told him of the fire in the night on top of the volcanoes of the Mountains of the Moon in the very heart of Africa. He listened as I explained how one milks a camel along the edge of the greatest of all deserts. But most of all, he listened to me tell of the people filling hundreds of new Nazarene churches across a vast area of Africa.

When I was finished, he cleared his voice and laughed. "Let me tell you of the beginning. The dawn when the very first African came in fear to your grandparents' wagon to ask them if they knew the way to the village of Jesus, and how far was it? Her name became Ruth, and her daughter was Marie. . . ."

He had seen the beginning, the lighting of the fire in the darkness of the African night!

Ten days later he was called to stand before the throne of the King and report it all. I know he did it in siSwati, and I think while the Master listened there were thousands of the old African preachers that he had known and worked with crowded around.

Have I not commanded you? Be strong and courageous. Do not be terrified; do not be discouraged, for the Lord your God will be with you wherever you go (Josh. 1:9, NIV).